Francis Frith's
WORCESTERSHIRE
LIVING MEMORIES

photographs of the mid twentieth century

Francis Frith's

WORCESTERSHIRE
LIVING MEMORIES

Dorothy Nicolle

FRITH
BOOK Co

First published in the United Kingdom in 2002 by
Frith Book Company Ltd

Hardback Edition 2002
ISBN 1-85937-489-1

British Library Cataloguing in Publication Data

Francis Frith's Worcestershire Living Memories
Dorothy Nicolle

Frith Book Company Ltd
Frith's Barn, Teffont,
Salisbury, Wiltshire SP3 5QP
Tel: +44 (0) 1722 716 376
Email: info@francisfrith.co.uk
www.francisfrith.co.uk

Printed and bound in Great Britain

Front Cover: Hereford & Worcester, Upton upon Severn, High Street c1955 U12022

contents

Francis Frith: Victorian Pioneer

FRANCIS FRITH, Victorian founder of the world-famous photographic archive, was a complex and multi-talented man. A devout Quaker and a highly successful Victorian businessman, he was both philosophic by nature and pioneering in outlook.

By 1855 Francis Frith had already established a wholesale grocery business in Liverpool, and sold it for the astonishing sum of £200,000, which is the equivalent today of over £15,000,000. Now a multi-millionaire, he was able to indulge his passion for travel. As a child he had pored over travel books written by early explorers, and his fancy and imagination had been stirred by family holidays to the sublime mountain regions of Wales and Scotland. 'What a land of spirit-stirring and enriching scenes and places!' he had written. He was to return to these scenes of grandeur in later years to 'recapture the thousands of vivid and tender memories', but with a different purpose. Now in his thirties, and captivated by the new science of photography, Frith set out on a series of pioneering journeys to the Nile regions that occupied him from 1856 until 1860.

Intrigue and Adventure

He took with him on his travels a specially-designed wicker carriage that acted as both dark-room and sleeping chamber. These far-flung journeys were packed with intrigue and adventure. In his life story, written when he was sixty-three, Frith tells of being held captive by bandits, and of fighting 'an awful midnight battle to the very point of surrender with a deadly pack of hungry, wild dogs'. Sporting flowing Arab costume, Frith arrived at Akaba by camel seventy years before Lawrence, where he encountered 'desert princes and rival sheikhs, blazing with jewel-hilted swords'.

During these extraordinary adventures he was assiduously exploring the desert regions bordering the Nile and patiently recording the antiquities and peoples with his camera. He was the first photographer to venture beyond the sixth cataract. Africa was still the mysterious 'Dark Continent', and Stanley and Livingstone's historic meeting was a decade into the future. The conditions for picture taking confound belief. He laboured for hours in his wicker dark-room in the sweltering heat of the desert, while the volatile chemicals fizzed dangerously in their trays. Often he was forced to work in remote tombs and caves where conditions were cooler. Back in London he exhibited his photographs and was 'rapturously cheered' by members of the Royal Society. His reputation as a photographer was made overnight. An eminent modern historian has likened their impact on the population of the time to that on our own generation of the first photographs taken on the surface of the moon.

Venture of a Life-Time

Characteristically, Frith quickly spotted the opportunity to create a new business as a specialist publisher of photographs. He lived in an era of immense and sometimes violent change. For the poor in the early part of Victoria's reign work was a drudge and the hours long, and people had precious little free time to enjoy themselves. Most had no transport other than a cart or gig at their disposal, and had not travelled far beyond the boundaries of their own town or village. However,

by the 1870s, the railways had threaded their way across the country, and Bank Holidays and half-day Saturdays had been made obligatory by Act of Parliament. All of a sudden the ordinary working man and his family were able to enjoy days out and see a little more of the world.

With characteristic business acumen, Francis Frith foresaw that these new tourists would enjoy having souvenirs to commemorate their days out. In 1860 he married Mary Ann Rosling and set out with the intention of photographing every city, town and village in Britain. For the next thirty years he travelled the country by train and by pony and trap, producing fine photographs of seaside resorts and beauty spots that were keenly bought by millions of Victorians. These prints were painstakingly pasted into family albums and pored over during the dark nights of winter, rekindling precious memories of summer excursions.

The Rise of Frith & Co

Frith's studio was soon supplying retail shops all over the country. To meet the demand he gathered about him a small team of photographers, and published the work of independent artist-photographers of the calibre of Roger Fenton and Francis Bedford. In order to gain some understanding of the scale of Frith's business one only has to look at the catalogue issued by Frith & Co in 1886: it runs to some 670 pages, listing not only many thousands of views of the British Isles but also many photographs of most European countries, and China, Japan, the USA and Canada – note the sample page shown above from the hand-written *Frith & Co* ledgers detailing pictures taken. By 1890 Frith had created the greatest specialist photographic publishing company in the

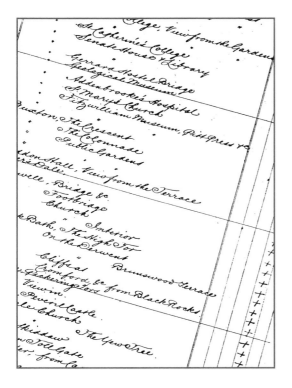

year after Frith's death, a new card measuring 5.5 x 3.5 inches became the standard format, but it was not until 1902 that the divided back came into being, with address and message on one face and a full-size illustration on the other. *Frith & Co* were in the vanguard of postcard development, and Frith's sons Eustace and Cyril continued their father's monumental task, expanding the number of views offered to the public and recording more and more places in Britain, as the coasts and countryside were opened up to mass travel.

Francis Frith died in 1898 at his villa in Cannes, his great project still growing. The archive he created continued in business for another seventy years. By 1970 it contained over a third of a million pictures of 7,000 cities, towns and villages. The massive photographic record Frith has left to us stands as a living monument to a special and very remarkable man.

world, with over 2,000 outlets – more than the combined number that Boots and W H Smith have today! The picture on the right shows the *Frith & Co* display board at Ingleton in the Yorkshire Dales. Beautifully constructed with mahogany frame and gilt inserts, it could display up to a dozen local scenes.

Postcard Bonanza

The ever-popular holiday postcard we know today took many years to develop. In 1870 the Post Office issued the first plain cards, with a pre-printed stamp on one face. In 1894 they allowed other publishers' cards to be sent through the mail with an attached adhesive halfpenny stamp. Demand grew rapidly, and in 1895 a new size of postcard was permitted called the court card, but there was little room for illustration. In 1899, a

Frith's Archive: A Unique Legacy

FRANCIS FRITH'S legacy to us today is of immense significance and value, for the magnificent archive of evocative photographs he created provides a unique record of change in 7,000 cities, towns and villages throughout Britain over a century and more. Frith and his fellow studio photographers revisited locations many times down the years to update their views, compiling for us an enthralling and colourful pageant of British life and character.

We tend to think of Frith's sepia views of Britain as nostalgic, for most of us use them to conjure up memories of places in our own lives with which we have family associations. It often makes us forget that to Francis Frith they were records of daily life as it was actually being lived in the cities, towns and villages of his day. The Victorian age was one of great and often bewildering change for ordinary people, and though the pictures evoke an impression of slower times, life was as busy and hectic as it is today.

We are fortunate that Frith was a photographer of the people, dedicated to recording the minutiae of everyday life. For it is this sheer wealth of visual data, the painstaking chronicle of changes in dress, transport, street layouts, buildings, housing, engineering and landscape that captivates us so much today. His remarkable images offer us a powerful link with the past and with the lives of our ancestors.

Today's Technology

Computers have now made it possible for Frith's many thousands of images to be accessed almost instantly. In the Frith archive today, each photograph is carefully 'digitised' then stored on a CD Rom. Frith archivists can locate a single photograph amongst thousands within seconds. Views can be catalogued and sorted under a variety of categories of place and content to the immediate benefit of researchers.

Inexpensive reference prints can be created for them at the touch of a mouse button, and a wide range of books and other printed materials assembled and published for a wider, more general readership - in the next twelve months over a hundred Frith local history titles will be published! The day-to-day workings of the archive are very different from how they were in Francis Frith's time: imagine the herculean task of sorting through eleven tons of glass negatives as Frith had to do to locate a particular sequence of pictures!

THE FRANCIS FRITH COLLECTION
Photographic publishers since 1860

HOME | PHOTO SEARCH | BOOKS | PORTFOLIO | GALLERY | MY CART
Products | History | Other Collections | Contact us | Help?

your town,
your village

365,000
photographs of 7,000 towns and villages, taken between 1860 & 1970.

The Frith Archive
The Frith Archive is the remarkable legacy of its energetic and visionary founder. Today, the Frith archive is the only nationally important archive of its kind still in private ownership.

The Collection is world-renowned for the extraordinary quality of its images.

The Gallery
This month The Frith Gallery features images from "Frith's Egypt".

News...

Image update complete.
An additional 5,000 images have been added and the quality of all images has now been improved.

Sample Chapters avaliable.
The first selection of sample chapters from the Frith Book Co.'s extensive range is now available. All are offered in Pdf format for easy downloading and viewing.

explore
FRITH
Search thousands of photographs from one of the worlds' great archives.

Town search
GO

County search
Select a county
GO

the **FRITH**gallery

See Frith at www.francisfrith.co.uk

Yet the archive still prides itself on maintaining the same high standards of excellence laid down by Francis Frith, including the painstaking cataloguing and indexing of every view.

It is curious to reflect on how the internet now allows researchers in America and elsewhere greater instant access to the archive than Frith himself ever enjoyed. Many thousands of individual views can be called up on screen within seconds on one of the Frith internet sites, enabling people living continents away to revisit the streets of their ancestral home town, or view places in Britain where they have enjoyed holidays. Many overseas researchers welcome the chance to view special theme selections, such as transport, sports, costume and ancient monuments.

We are certain that Francis Frith would have heartily approved of these modern developments in imaging techniques, for he himself was always working at the very limits of Victorian photographic technology.

The Value of the Archive Today

Because of the benefits brought by the computer, Frith's images are increasingly studied by social historians, by researchers into genealogy and ancestory, by architects, town planners, and by teachers and schoolchildren involved in local history projects.

In addition, the archive offers every one of us an opportunity to examine the places where we and our families have lived and worked down the years. Highly successful in Frith's own era, the archive is now, a century and more on, entering a new phase of popularity.

The Past in Tune with the Future

Historians consider the Francis Frith Collection to be of prime national importance. It is the only archive of its kind remaining in private ownership and has been valued at a million pounds. However, this figure is now rapidly increasing as digital technology enables more and more people around the world to enjoy its benefits.

Francis Frith's archive is now housed in an historic timber barn in the beautiful village of Teffont in Wiltshire. Its founder would not recognize the archive office as it is today. In place of the many thousands of dusty boxes containing glass plate negatives and an all-pervading odour of photographic chemicals, there are now ranks of computer screens. He would be amazed to watch his images travelling round the world at unimaginable speeds through network and internet lines.

The archive's future is both bright and exciting. Francis Frith, with his unshakeable belief in making photographs available to the greatest number of people, would undoubtedly approve of what is being done today with his lifetime's work. His photographs, depicting our shared past, are now bringing pleasure and enlightenment to millions around the world a century and more after his death.

Worcestershire Living Memories
An Introduction

All places can be said to be ancient, but Worcestershire truly is. It is especially ancient in geological terms because the Malvern Hills are amongst the oldest rocks, if not in Britain then certainly in England. They are at least 650 million years old. It has been claimed that from these hills 15 counties of England and Wales can be viewed. Whether that is true or not, they certainly provide a wonderful vantage point for viewing a large expanse of the county of Worcestershire, rising as they do to almost 1400 feet.

Worcestershire has been described as being rather like a pie-crust, with lowland in the centre and hills all around the rim with a few breaks where the major rivers cut through. The Malverns form the westernmost crust of this imaginary pie with the River Teme to their north, beyond which lie the Abberley Hills. These are in turn cut off by the Severn and Stour rivers, before the northern crust is marked by the Clent and Lickey Hills. To the north-east there is another break in the crust: here the valley of the Avon cuts through, before the eastern boundary of the county is marked by the beginnings of the Cotswolds. The southern boundary of the county opens up into the wide Severn valley with outcrops of hills, such as Bredon Hill in the far south.

Many of these boundary hills are topped with

Iron Age hill-forts. Early man saw the benefits, too, of such high vantage points with their excellent views of the countryside around. Today the best survivor of these hill-forts is the one known as the British Camp on the Malvern Hills. Those early Britons also gave the county its name - Worcestershire. When the Saxons arrived in Britannia they named the town that we now know as Worcester after the local tribe called the Weogora. It is thought that the name of the Wyre Forest in the north-west of the county comes from the same root. Not that we know what it means! There are suggestions that it refers to 'the people who lived by the winding river', a reference perhaps to the River Severn, but it is unlikely that we will ever know for certain.

When the Saxons arrived and started to settle here from the 6th and 7th centuries, they found a landscape that was dotted with small Roman settlements. In fact in Roman times Droitwich, with its salt works, was probably the most important town in the area; Worcester was then a relatively small fort guarding a crossing point over the River Severn. But it was the importance of the safe river crossing acting as a focus for travellers (and therefore traders) that led to the growth of Worcester, so much so that by the end of the 7th century a cathedral had been established here. From then on the city rapidly expanded, and by medieval times it had become one of the most important cities in England.

Worcester's moment of glory, however, was to occur in the 17th century during the Civil War - not that it would have seemed particularly glorious at the time. The city supported the King: it is proud that it was the first in the country to declare its support, and then the last to surrender in 1646 after a siege of two months. Five years later, it was to become a battlefield when the uncrowned King Charles II and his Scots army tried to hold the city against Oliver Cromwell's Roundheads. Charles only just managed to escape, and eventually made his way to France. It was as a result of its loyalty to the Stuart cause that Worcester became known as 'The Faithful City'; to this day an effigy of Cromwell can be seen nailed above the door of the Guildhall.

Worcester people could be said to have had an interest in politics from early times, so much so that the world's oldest surviving newspaper, the 'Worcester Journal', was founded here in 1690. It was established with the definite purpose of encouraging support for the new King and Queen, William and Mary, and issues of the paper were sold as far afield as Gloucester, Bridgnorth and Warwick. Costing 2d, it was not merely a local newspaper; rather, it concentrated on news from outside the region. In the mid 1700s, a rival newspaper, also calling

itself the 'Worcester Journal', was established, and so Harvey Berrow, the proprietor at the time, renamed his paper Berrow's Worcester Journal (the name it has to this day) so that customers would know which was the genuine article.

This century was to see the growth of Worcester both as a commercial and social centre. The famous Three Choirs Festival, with the cathedral choirs of Worcester, Gloucester and Hereford alternating as hosts for the event, dates from this time. Also dating from around the same period is the world-famous Royal Worcester china company. It was founded in 1751, and very soon acquired a reputation for the high quality of its porcelain, a reputation it maintains to this day. One of the founders of the company was Dr John Wall, a very keen amateur artist. The doctor was also a founder of the Worcester Royal Infirmary, and carried out research on the medical properties of the spring water that issued from the Malvern Hills, hence the little rhyme:

'Malvern Water, says Dr John Wall
Is famous for containing nothing at all'.

But Worcestershire does not just consist of the city of Worcester. For centuries the city served as the religious and trading centre for all the smaller communities around it. Traditionally the economy of those communities had been largely rural. 'This is the land of apples, plums and pears.' The Vale of Evesham in the south-east of Worcestershire contains some of the most fertile soil in the country, suitable for growing all kinds of crops. It was only relatively recently, towards the end of the 17th century in fact, that a Genoan called Francis Bernardi introduced the commercial cultivation of vegetables to the area, thus starting the concentration on the fruit and vegetables for which it is now famous. Today the region around Evesham and westwards towards Pershore could be described as a 'vegetable factory' producing salad vegetables, peas, beans and especially asparagus for dinner tables around the country.

The 18th century was to see the beginnings of changes of a different nature throughout the country. In nearby Shropshire the Industrial Revolution took off. Soon the effects of the changes brought about there were to become apparent in the towns of Wolverhampton, Dudley and Birmingham, giving rise to the term 'the Black Country' with which we are so familiar today. These changes were soon to be seen in Worcestershire towns, particularly in Redditch and Bromsgrove, where the small iron forges that already existed were soon to expand. Needle-making, using wire produced in nearby Birmingham, for example, was

already a major cottage industry in Redditch in the late 1700s. In 1828 the first steam-driven needle mill was established, and within sixty years 10,000 people in the town were producing around 50 million needles and 20 million fish hooks each week.

You can produce all the needles you like, but they are worthless unless they can reach your customers. The 18th century was also to see an enormous change in communications around Britain, first of all with the development of an effective road system using the new toll roads and then with the introduction of canals. Worcestershire benefited from this too, particularly with the building of the Staffordshire and Worcestershire Canal. This linked producers in the north of the county, and also those in the Black Country and the Potteries, with markets all over Britain, and also with any foreign markets that could be reached from ports such as Bristol and Liverpool.

There was one tiny little hamlet that was really to benefit from the building of this particular canal. Originally, the plan was that the canal would link with the River Severn at Bewdley; but the traders there were doing very nicely, thank you, and did not see how a 'stinking ditch' would be of any benefit to them. So the canal was built to join the Severn some miles downstream. Thus Stourport on Severn suddenly began to thrive, not only with the

trade the canal brought, but with industry too. It soon outgrew Bewdley. It did mean, however, that the 'beautiful place' stayed beautiful; in fact, in the 21st century Bewdley is something of a Georgian time-warp of a town.

Nearby Kidderminster was also to develop from the industrial age and the introduction of canals. Today the town is associated with the production of carpets, but originally any weaving done here had been associated with the weaving of woollen cloth. The first looms for carpets, hand-looms in those days, were set up in the mid 1700s by a man called John Broom; he was to make (and lose) three fortunes while trying to establish this business. When power-looms were introduced here, also in 1828, there were riots amongst the workers at what they saw as a potential loss of work. But the power-looms stayed, and the town's reputation for its carpets grew - Kidderminster's carpets were famous for their durability and brilliant colours, which were said to stem from the special properties of the water of the River Stour on which the town sat.

In the years after the Second World War, the time when all the photographs in this collection were taken, the towns of the industrial north of Worcestershire began to see a decline in their industrial base. Today a large proportion of the population works in service industries, and

amongst these, tourism has become very important. This was a process that started in the 19th century, and was foreseen by people such as the photographer Francis Frith. It led to the development particularly of towns such as Malvern, that catered for visitors from far and near not only with its historic and artistic interest, but with its access to magnificent countryside as well. Today Malvern is renowned not only for its Priory but also as an important centre for the arts with its Malvern Festival,

which is held each year.

Worcestershire is a truly ancient county - but time never stands still, and changes continue to take place, not least political changes. As recently as the 1970s, Worcestershire was 'married' to Herefordshire to form a single county. But it was very much a shot-gun marriage - neither party was happy about the situation - and the inevitable divorce followed in 1998. Worcestershire is once again a county in its own right.

Worcester
The County Capital

Worcester
The Cathedral from the River c1960 W141042
This is a view that should be familiar to all those of us lucky enough to have a £20 note in our pockets. The cathedral is closely associated with the composer, Edward Elgar, who is also shown on the note. Incidentally, the Georgian house beside the cathedral is the only privately-owned building in the country ever to have featured on a British banknote.

**Worcester
High Street c1950** W141015
The Guildhall stands in the
High Street, just behind the
iron gateway shown here on
the left of the street. Today the
High Street is totally
pedestrianised. The buildings
remain much the same,
although the one on the far left
has been replaced.

**Worcester
The Guildhall c1965** W141073
The wonderfully ornate façade of
the Guildhall has statues of Charles
I, Charles II and Queen Anne, and
written above the door are the
words 'may the faithful city flourish'.
This is a reminder of the loyal
support given by the city to the
Royalist cause during the Civil War.
There is also a carved head of Oliver
Cromwell above the door, with nails
through his ears!

Worcester, The Cross c1950 W141018
The Cross is so-named because there was once an old market cross here; it was on this spot that
Elizabeth I was greeted on her arrival in the city in 1574. St Nicholas's church in the centre of the
picture was built in 1730, but today is used as a bar! Notice the tramlines above the street.

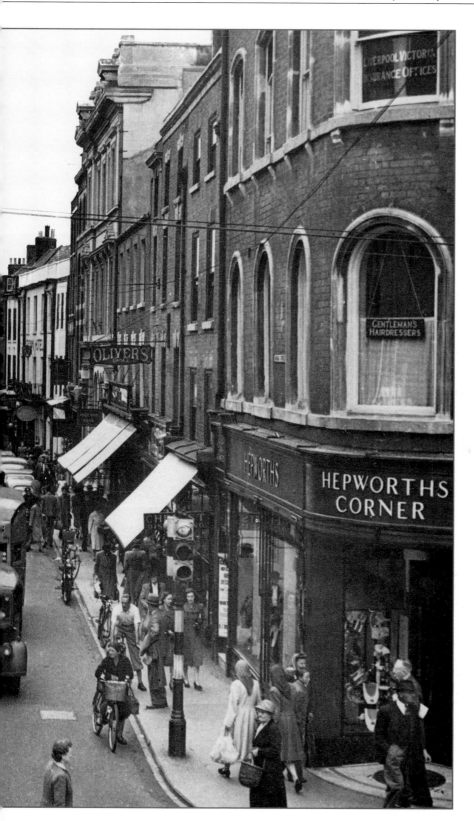

**Worcester
Broad Street c1950**
W141022
A large part of the
centre of the city of
Worcester is now either
closed to traffic or has
restricted access, and
even as early as 1950
we can see in this
photograph how the
congestion was
developing. Buildings
are still recognisable
here, but at the far end
of Broad Street,
however, there has
been massive
redevelopment with
the building of the
Crowngate Shopping
Centre.

**Worcester
Angel Place c1950**
W141037
This is a most unusual
Francis Frith
photograph, for it
shows a rainy day.
Judging by the
photographs in the
archive, it would seem
that it is always summer
when a Frith
photographer is
present. The steeple is
known locally as the
Glover's Needle
because it is so slender
- glove making was
once a major industry
here.

▲ Worcester
Friar Street c1950
W141013
'There be divers faire strets in the towne well buyldyd with tymbar.' So wrote Leland when he visited in the 16th century. Friar Street is delightful with its mishmash of buildings from all periods. Particularly fine is Greyfriars, jutting out on the right, which dates from 1480 and is now looked after by the National Trust.

Worcester ▶
King Charles II House
New Street c1965
W141076
The sign to the right of the door reads 'From this house King Charles II escaped his enemies after the Battle of Worcester, September 3 1651'. In fact he escaped through a door at the back, which led directly on to the city walls. Today the house has a third storey, but this has in no way detracted from its charm.

▲ Powick
The Roundabout c1955
P108002
Worcester saw the last battle of the Civil War. It could also be said to have seen the first military engagement nine years earlier - a skirmish took place when a group of Parliamentary soldiers were surprised by the river at nearby Powick and routed by Prince Rupert and his men. Parliamentary accounts admit to the loss of 37 men, although the death toll was probably higher.

◄ **Hallow**
The Village c1955
H152006
Queen Elizabeth I once stayed at Hallow on one of her royal progresses around the country. Her retinue was so large that it included 1,500 horses. This must have been a terrible expense for the people who lived in cottages such as this. The cottage has gone now, to be replaced by two modern houses, but the telephone kiosk still remains.

Hallow, The Green c1955 H152007
Hallow is a small village just to the north-west of Worcester; it is so close to the city that it could really almost be termed a suburb. With the new buildings that such villages generate, it is a pleasure to find that this village green still survives, even if it does have a much more manicured appearance these days.

Hallow, The Post Office and Oakleigh Avenue c1955 H152001
The house on the left was (and still is) Hallow's post office. Today, however, it has grown, with an extension to the right of the building; in order to accommodate customers, much of the grass verge in the foreground has been taken over by parking space.

The Industrial North-East of Worcestershire

Blakedown
Birmingham Road c1965 B419011
Like so many, this junction tends to be much busier in the
middle of the day now than when it was photographed in the
mid 1960s. Blakedown sits on the road that links Kidderminster
with Birmingham. Notice the sign on the board beside the
grocer's shop - it advertises a village fete.

Clent
Early Morning over the Clent Hills c1955 C330007
Clent is an old English word for a rocky hill. This rock formation,
however, is not quite as old as the hills, nor are the rocks a genuine
ancient monument. They are known locally as the Four Stones, and it
somehow comes as no surprise that they have only been standing here
like this for a few hundred rather than a few thousand years.

Clent, The Village from the Clent Hills c1955 C330001
There are magnificent views from the Clent Hills in all directions. The village is one that really does seem to nestle amongst its hills; to reach it we need to follow lots of narrow, twisting little lanes that seem to lead in all directions and then suddenly come to the village.

Clent, The Village c1965 C330015
Notice all the piles of paving stones waiting to be laid into the pavement. Such a photograph could never have been very successful as a postcard had it been sold in the village, but it serves to remind us of the use of the Francis Frith photographic collection as an archive of everyday life in Britain through these years and for the future.

Belbroughton
High Street c1965 B418006
This is quite an attractive little village, with one or two very fine
18th-century houses. Like so many small villages locally, it had
close links with the industry of the Black Country to the north -
here they were famous for the production of scythes, an
important tool in a largely rural community.

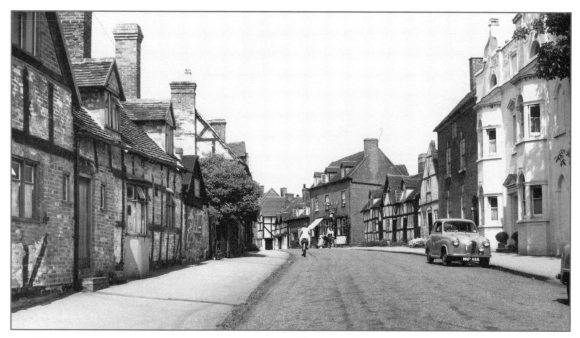

Chaddesley Corbett, The Village c1960 C328002
The village of Chaddesley Corbett sits just beside, but off, the main road linking Kidderminster and Bromsgrove, and so retains its charm; it has numerous delightful Tudor and Georgian buildings. Today, however, the timber-framed buildings do look in a much better condition with fresh white paint over the brickwork.

Chaddesley Corbett, Harvington Hall c1960 K16066
A mile or two outside the village sits Harvington Hall. It is a wonderfully evocative Tudor mansion surrounded by a moat, which we see here. Said to have the largest number of priest holes of any building in England, the hall is now owned by the Roman Catholic Archdiocese of Birmingham. It is used as a religious educational centre, and is open to the public each summer.

Rubery, Main Road c1965 R260028
In Rubery we are far from the 'pastoral heart of England', a phrase which was used by Quiller-Couch to describe Eckington in the south of Worcestershire. Here we are physically and emotionally much more closely linked with Birmingham and the Black Country than with Worcester or even the county of Worcestershire.

◀ **Barnt Green
The Village c1965**
B417004
Barnt Green is a rare village in this series in that instead of the number of shops on the main street declining, here they have actually increased. For example, in this photograph the private houses on the far right have now been converted into shops, and the hedges have been removed to give easy access.

◄ Barnt Green
The Village c1960
B417005
Although it is in
Worcestershire, the
village of Barnt Green
could, like Rubery,
almost be described as
being part of
Birmingham today. Most
of the people who live
here will work in
Birmingham, travelling
up daily from the railway
station in the village.

▼ Lickey, Lickey Hills
Amusement Park c1965
L215022
The Lickey Hills area has been
a traditional focus for leisure
activities since 1888, when part
of the present 524-acre park
was presented to the City of
Birmingham. Today the leisure
activities focus on the walks
through the forest and the
wildlife in the area, and there is
an excellent Visitor Centre.
There is also an 18-hole golf
course within the country park.

◄ Lickey
The View from the
Beacon c1965 L215013
The Lickey Hills consist
of some of the oldest
rock in Britain. At 975 ft
above sea level, Beacon
Hill provides a
magnificent view of just
about all of Birmingham
(the second largest city
in Great Britain). Is the
group shown in the
photograph here to
study the area, or are
they simply enjoying
that wonderful view?

Lickey, The Monument c1965 L215011
Today the trees are as high as the monument! It was erected in the 1830s to commemorate the 'disinterested, solid and efficient public services' of the 6th Earl of Plymouth. 'Disinterested' seems an odd word to use, but these days few people recognise that there is a difference between 'uninterested' and 'disinterested', which means something entirely different - the Earl's services were unbiased, impartial or unselfish.

Bromsgrove, High Street c1960 B233045
'The towne of Bromsgrove is all in a manner of one street, very long' was a description of this area some 400 years ago. Following the industrial revolution in the 18th century, the town developed rapidly; it became famous for its production of buttons and nails. Other things were made here too, including the iron gates that now surround Buckingham Palace.

Bromsgrove
High Street c1950 B233005
It is a puzzle sometimes with these pictures to work out what
survives and what has gone. For instance, the Midland Bank, in
the centre, looks very different today, although it survives as the
HSBC: the ground floor windows have now all been changed into
an open arcade giving shelter from the elements to customers
entering and leaving the bank within.

◄ **Beoley, The Post Office c1965** B845002
The name of this village is actually pronounced 'Beeley', and presumably honey production was once important here. Today the village's main claim to fame is its connection to the Sheldon family, whose tombs are in the local church. William Sheldon introduced tapestry weaving to England in the late 15th century, and Sheldon tapestries are very rare and very valuable.

◄ **Bromsgrove, High Street c1950** B233009
Much of the High Street is now closed to traffic. There is a particularly fine statue halfway along the street which commemorates Bromsgrove's most famous son, the poet A E Housman. He looks as though he is about to go striding across the Shropshire hills nearby. They were the inspiration for much of his work, the best known of which is 'The Shropshire Lad'.

**Bromsgrove, Ye Olde ►
Shoppe and the
Church c1950**
B233007
This is an interesting photograph because although the building that houses Appleby's, the ironmongers, still survives, the building next door has been replaced. Also, the road level has since been raised at this corner, so that now the pavement here is a couple of feet below that of the road.

◄ **Redditch
Market Place c1965**
R84044
Redditch was once exactly that - it was described as 'Le Red Dych' in a document in 1300. Why it should have been red is difficult to understand, although it might have been intended to mean 'the reed ditch'. The Market Place shown here has now been completely pedestrianised, with stalls for a weekly market occupying what was once the road.

▼ Redditch, Alcester Street c1960 R84041

If you have not visited Redditch in the last 40 years, you will now be quite unable to find your way around. The heart of the town has been totally surrounded by a new ring road, which has completely slashed its way through all the buildings in the foreground of this picture.

▼ Redditch, Evesham Street c1955 R84008

Just like Alcester Street in picture No R84041, Evesham Street is now a truncated little road that leads nowhere. It was once a busy, bustling part of Redditch - but not any longer. Notice the delivery cart parked on the left of the road.

▲ Redditch, Evesham Street c1960 R84039

From a tiny little settlement surrounded by a red ditch, by the 19th century Redditch had become an important industrial town famous for its production of needles and fishing hooks. In the 20th century it was also famous for the production of bicycles. Notice that the bollard in the 1955 picture, No R84008, is marked by a patch of tarmac in this one!

◀ **Redditch**
The Lakes
Blatchley Estate c1960
R84035
This is typical of many new estates around towns in the Midlands in the 1960s. It is still quite close to the centre of the old town, which is marked by the spire of St Stephen's church on the right-hand side.

▼ Astwood Bank, Edgioake Lane c1965 A163003

'Greensleeves' is now the name of the thatched house on the right. It is a typical example of how many of Worcestershire's black-and-white buildings have evolved over the years. Today it is all one private house, but originally it would have comprised a number of little adjoining cottages.

▼ Stoke Prior, The Canal c1965 H501009

This view shows one of the locks on the Birmingham Canal, which was built to carry goods between Birmingham and Worcester and also to link up with traders on the River Severn. Notice the number of narrow boats waiting to go through the lock. By this time some of them would have already been carrying holidaymakers rather than transporting goods.

**▲ Wychbold
St Mary-de-Wych
Church c1950** W311001
The word 'wych' in this context probably refers to an early trading centre (a similar use of the word is Aldwych in London). However, the term 'wich' in Droitwich, the town a couple of miles to the south, refers to the salt works there (we find the same word in the names of other salt producing towns such as Nantwich and Middlewich, for example, in Cheshire).

◀ **Wychbold**
The Crown Hotel c1950
W311003
The Crown Hotel, pictured here, is typical of many that were built in the middle years of the 20th century to cater for a population that was newly mobile, thanks to the availability of cars. It still serves exactly the same purpose today, although it has been taken over and has now changed its name. The sign at the far end of the car park tells us that in the 1950s the hotel had a swimming pool.

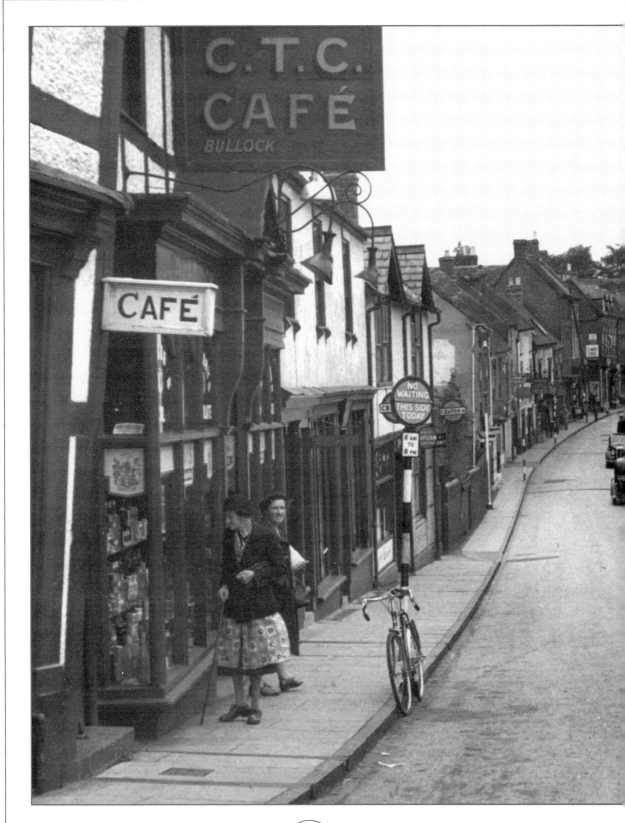

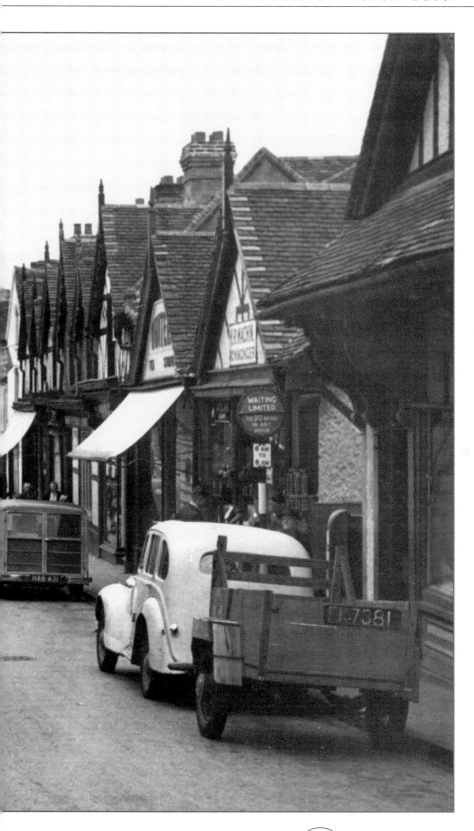

**Droitwich
High Street c1955**
D54040
The name Droitwich actually means 'the dirty salt works'. In Roman times, Droitwich was called 'Salinae' because of the importance of its salt springs; they contain 40 per cent more salt than the Dead Sea. From early times salt has been essential as a preservative of foodstuffs during long winters. Our word 'salary' is derived from the fact that Roman soldiers were partly paid in salt.

Droitwich
High Street c1955 D54007
The building on the left is now used as office premises for the
Wychavon District Council. At the time of the photograph, it was used
as a café which catered particularly for the CTC, the Cyclists Touring
Club. Notice that the shop across the road has bicycle wheels in the
windows. Presumably Mr Roberts also sold puncture repair kits and
the like for potential customers stopping for tea across the road.

North-Western Worcestershire and the Severn & Teme Rivers

Kidderminster
The Policeman 1957 K16031
If we stand at this spot today, the only thing shown in the photograph that we will still find is the Georgian building in the background, behind the statue. The heart of Kidderminster has been totally rebuilt; yet, unlike the disaster that Redditch has become, this town still has a certain style and personality. It has not lost its heart.

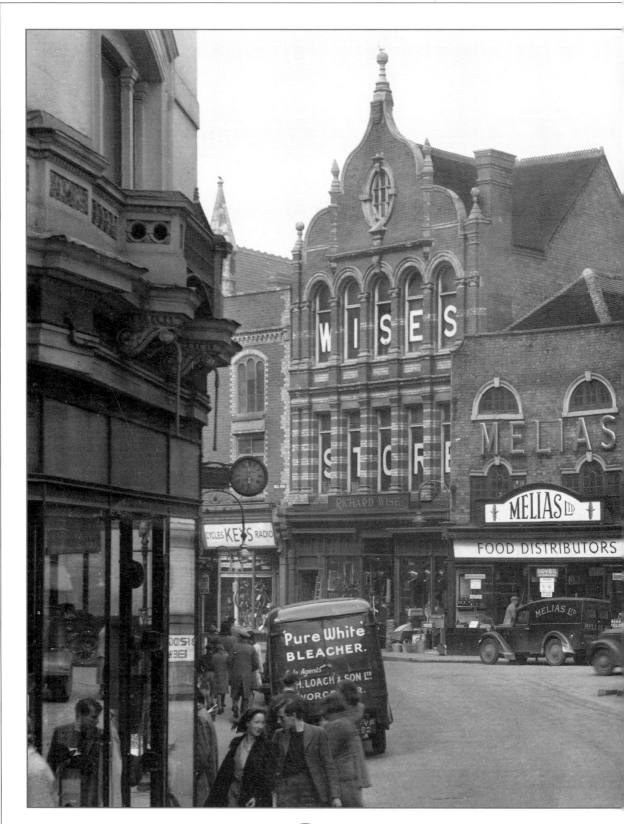

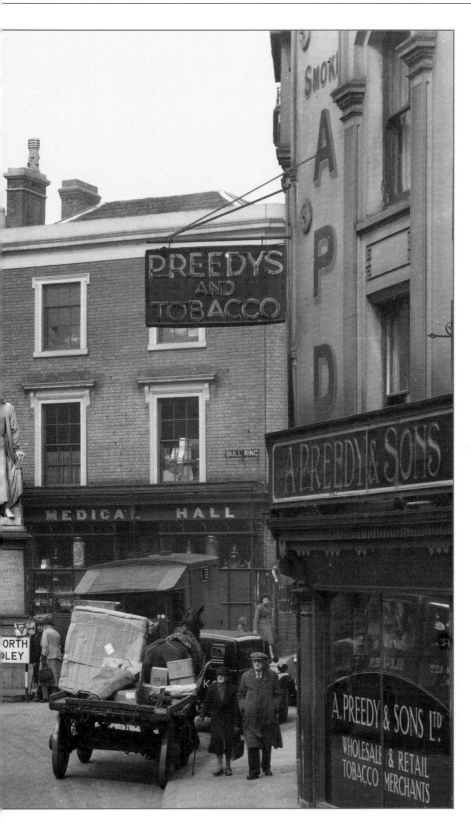

**Kidderminster
The Bull Ring c1950**
K16001
Again, most of the buildings we see here have been replaced. The Bull Ring marks the end of the pedestrianised area, so we can still see cars and vans here. But we are unlikely now to see a horse-drawn cart parked outside the shops waiting to collect goods for delivery.

Kidderminster, The Baxter Statue c1955 K16011
The statue of Richard Baxter has been moved, and now stands outside St Mary and All Saints' Church. Baxter was a preacher in the 17th century; he once said that in Kidderminster there were 'few beggars because their common trade of stuff-weaving would find work for all'. He was referring to the cloth weaving trade; carpet weaving was not introduced to the town until the 1700s.

Kidderminster, Vicar Street c1950 K16002
Another man associated with Kidderminster stands outside the Town Hall at the end of Vicar Street. Rowland Hill was born into a poor family in a time when people dreaded a postman's knock on the door: at that time you had to pay for the delivery of any letter you received. In 1840 he introduced the Penny Post, whereby the person posting a letter was responsible for the cost of its delivery.

Kidderminster, Vicar Street c1960 K16062
Vicar Street is also now free of traffic, but otherwise it is much the same as it is in this photograph. The clock (top left) is fixed to the corner of the Town Hall. The street here is really dominated by the wonderfully Italianate-style building on the left with its multi-coloured brickwork. Even the side of the building, which we can see clearly here, is decorated.

Shatterford, Main Road c1955 S384002
The Main Road is the main road linking Kidderminster and Bridgnorth, the A442, and today it is much wider and very much busier than it appears here. The building in the centre of the group is a pub called the Bellman's Cross, now painted white.

Cookley, Lea Castle Gates c1955 C333022
This very grand entrance sits on the main road that links Kidderminster with Woverhampton just beside the junction to Cookley. It still exists, and although there is now a tarmac drive through the gateway, the building itself has become very overgrown with ivy instead of roses. There are three girls sitting on the pavement - perhaps they are waiting for a bus.

▼ **Cookley, The Recreation Ground c1965** C333027
Cookley is a rather over-grown village overlooking the River Stour; since the 1700s, it has also overlooked the Staffordshire and Worcestershire Canal, which links Stourport and Kidderminster with Wolverhampton and the Black Country to the north. Notice the canopies on the two prams; they were once a very common feature, but now we have plastic cocoons over pushchairs instead!

▼ **Cookley, The Square c1955** C333017
This scene has changed quite considerably. The building in the centre with the white-framed doorway has a sign telling us that it is the Eagle at Cookley. The building has now gone, but the pub has moved next door. The trees have gone, sad to say, and the road is framed with yellow lines telling us where we can (and more often cannot) park.

▲ **Cookley, The Village School c1965** C333045
It is obviously time for the children in the playground to stop playing with their friends and go home. All their elder brothers and sisters are waiting patiently to collect them.

◀ Upper Arley, The Ferry and the Village c1955

A164001

Upper Arley has been described as 'the loveliest hamlet on the Severn'; it really is extremely pretty, attracting many visitors on even a cold winter's day. It is an excellent point from which to start a river-side walk, as there is a footbridge here and further bridges within about three or four miles both upstream and downstream, with delightful paths along the way.

◀ **Upper Arley, The Ferry and the Village c1955**
A164060
Notice the castle tower. It was part of Arley Castle, built in 1844 as a Dower House for the Lyttleton family of Hagley Hall. At this time Arley on Severn, as it was then called, was still part of Staffordshire; it was absorbed by Worcestershire (the county boundary is about a mile to the north) in 1895. The castle has since been demolished.

Upper Arley
The River and the Village
c1960 A164058
In the 1950s and 60s, however, you still had to cross the river on the ferry or the punt. A ferry was first recorded as being in use here in 1323, and when the idea for a footbridge was first mooted, there was a great deal of local opposition. But the ferry had really become too expensive to run, and the bridge was built in 1971.

Bewdley
The Bridge c1960 B82044
The bridge here is one of a number of bridges over the Severn designed by the famous Scottish engineer, Thomas Telford; it cost £11,000. The previous bridge was destroyed in the 'Great Flood' of 1795, which was higher than any flood recorded since! Sad to say, the grandstand here has disappeared.

Bewdley, Severnside
North c1965 B82062
The name Bewdley comes from the English pronunciation of the French words 'beau lieu', meaning 'beautiful place', and was given to the settlement by the Normans. It is particularly beautiful along the banks by the Severn, but the people who live here must wonder sometimes if beauty is everything - when the Severn floods, the water regularly enters their houses.

**Bewdley
Load Street c1950**

B82031

It was in Bewdley that Henry VII's eldest son, Arthur, married Catherine of Aragon. They were married by proxy: a man from the Spanish court stood in for Catherine, who was still in Spain. After they finally met, the couple went to live in Ludlow, where Arthur soon died. His funeral procession passed through Bewdley on the way to Worcester, where he was buried in the cathedral.

◀ **Bewdley**
The Caravan Park
c1955 B82039
This caravan park is just upstream of the town (the River Severn is defined by the line of trees at the end of the field). Today the caravans have all been replaced by much grander, well-established, static caravans, many with their own gardens.

Bewdley
Load Street c1955 B82021

This view shows the close connection of the town with the river. Bewdley was an important trading centre where road traffic met river traffic. Before a bridge was built here, there was a ferry crossing. The name 'load' is thought to be an Old English word meaning 'ferry'. In 1425 the Bewdley ferry business was valued at the enormous sum of £5 a year.

▼ Ribbesford, Blackstone
Rock c1965 R269008

We are downstream from Bewdley, and the course of the River Severn can again be defined in this photograph by the line of trees. The rock formation on the opposite bank of the river is a soft sandstone into which caves were cut long ago; it was once used as a hermitage.

◄ Ribbesford
The Lido Café c1965
R269005

The building for this little café still exists, but it has since been converted into a pub - the Woodman.

Stourport-on-Severn
Distant View c1955 S214020
Stourport sits at the point where the River Stour enters the River
Severn, but the settlement here only developed after the building
of the Staffordshire and Worcestershire Canal in 1771. Neither
Bridgnorth nor Bewdley (both much more important towns
originally) wanted a canal link ('a stinking ditch') and so Stourport
was to benefit from their short-sightedness.

Stourport-on-Severn, Bridge Street c1955 S214024
This street scene has changed little over the last 50 years, although the large Post Office building has gone (to be replaced by a ghastly 1960s shop front). The town developed as a trading and industrial centre because of the importance of the canal, but it has since declined and now depends largely on visitors.

Stourport-on-Severn, Bridge Street c1965 S214047
This photograph must have been taken at the height of the holiday season because the shop on the right, M A Grinnall's, has a number of beach balls and inflatable air beds on display outside. I don't know where they were intended to be used - the currents of the River Severn are notoriously dangerous.

▼ **Stourport-on-Severn, The River c1955** S214030
This photograph and No S214070 are particularly interesting
because both views are taken from exactly the same spot on the
Stourport Bridge. Notice that there are some boats moored,
obviously available for hire.

▼ **Stourport-on-Severn, The River Severn c1965** S214070
By the mid 1960s the boat hire business has boomed, judging from this
photograph. Also the pleasure boat rides are increasingly popular, as they are to
this day. Notice the white ticket booth beside the ramp. Today there is a proper
building on the opposite side of the path where you buy your tickets.

▲ **Stourport-on-Severn
The Promenade c1965**
S214054
This is the view looking
back towards the bridge.
It would appear that
there is a queue of
people waiting to buy
tickets for a ride on the
pleasure boat. Notice,
just beyond them, the
spiral staircase leading
onto the bridge.

◄ **Stourport-on-Severn
The River Downstream from
the Bridge c1965** S214051
Because of its position on the
banks of the river, and
because of its proximity to
Kidderminster, Birmingham
and the Black Country,
Stourport became an
important leisure centre in the
19th century. Today this
aspect of the town continues;
there is now a large
amusement park where the
Riverside Café stands in this
photograph. Also the view is
no longer marred by those
enormous chimneys, which
have all come down.

▼ Stourport-on-Severn, The Weir c1965 S214045

This weir is about two miles downstream of the confluence of the Stour and Severn Rivers. Both Stour and Severn are very old river names, probably Celtic. It is interesting that there are five rivers in England called Stour; the name is thought to mean 'the strong one'. What the name Severn means, however, is anyone's guess.

▼ Ombersley, The Traffic Island c1955 O18003

Fortunately ,Ombersley is now by-passed by the main Worcester to Kidderminster road to the east, and so it survives as an extremely pretty little village with numerous delightful black-and-white buildings. Notice the crest on the gable end of this building; details like this can be seen on a number of the old houses here.

▲ Ombersley The Village c1955

O18006

Here we see another building with a crest on it, an intertwined S design - for the Sandys family. One member of the family was Bishop of Worcester, then Bishop of London, and finally Archbishop of York. A plaque over the centre of this house tells us that it was rebuilt in 1841. Fortunately, the Victorians didn't change the delightful character of the house.

◄ **Ombersley**
The King's Arms c1955
O18005
Ombersley is only a few miles north of Worcester, and it was in this direction that Charles II fled after the Battle of Worcester in 1651. While on the run, he is reputed to have stopped briefly at the (appropriately named) King's Arms, which we can see on the right here.

◀ **Ombersley
The Village c1955**
O18008
The large white building (centre) was known as the Crown Hotel then. Now called the Crown and Sandys Arms, it has a dubious claim to fame - a pop group called the Quarrymen once came here to perform, only to be thrown out because they were 'too scruffy'. Soon afterwards the group changed its name: it is now better known to history as the Beatles.

◄ Ombersley
The Village c1965
O18042
Amongst the buildings on the left of the road is a former Charity School. It has a wonderful plaque which tells us that the school taught reading, English, writing and arithmetic only to those children whose parents were worth less than £5 a year. How values have changed!

▼ Holt Fleet, The Wharf Hotel
c1955 H103024
The Beatles may have been thrown out of Ombersley, but the Rolling Stones played here. The low extension on the left was a very early disco where they once performed. The veranda around the main building of the pub has since been enclosed with large picture windows, giving a spacious dining area for customers.

◄ Holt Fleet, The Wharf Hotel Camping Site
c1955 H103046
Today the caravan park still lies just behind the Wharf Hotel; it is now solely for static caravans, owned mostly by people who live in Birmingham. Notice how even in the 1950s people were already using static caravans. Some even have fencing around their little gardens.

◄ **Holt Fleet, The Bridge c1955** H103023
This bridge, like the one at Bewdley, was designed by Thomas Telford; it replaced an old ferry and ford. It is a single-span iron bridge. When it opened in 1828, it was originally a toll bridge, although tolls no longer had to be paid after 1900.

◄ **Holt Fleet, The Locks c1955** H103059

The River Severn was traditionally one of the busiest trading routes in Britain, but travel could be severely restricted in time of flood or drought. With the introduction of canals in the 18th century to link the rivers, and even of locks on the rivers themselves, as shown here, the transportation of goods and people around the country became much more reliable.

▲ **Holt Fleet**
Holt Castle c1955

H103019

Holt Castle is a private house with wonderful views looking east over the Severn Valley. On the left we can see the branches of a Lebanon cedar. It is one of a pair of trees, both of which still survive, that have recently been dated: they are almost 200 years old, and would have been planted at the time when Napoleon Bonaparte ruled France.

Great Witley ►
Witley Court Church
c1960 G143006

Great Witley church has been described as 'the least English-looking church in Worcestershire'. It has an interior which is baroque in the extreme; much of the detail of the stucco decoration is actually made of papier-mâché. It is thought that Handel once played on the organ, which came originally from the Duke of Chandos' estate in Edgware.

◄ **Abberley**
The Village c1955
A255054
This is an old view of the main road linking Worcester and Tenbury Wells. What appears to be a really pretty little bus shelter just beside the car was actually the covering for an old well; it has since been removed.

Great Witley
The Village School
c1960 G143011
When the great house was built at Witley Court, the old village was in the way, and so it was moved here to its new position a mile away. Unlike many similarly small villages, however, it does still have its primary school.

Abberley ▶
The Clock Tower
c1955 A255010
'Jones's Folly' stands 161 feet high, and it makes a wonderful landmark which can be seen from miles away. It is named after the local squire, who built it over 100 years ago.

◀ **Abberley**
Abberley Hall
the Swimming Pool
c1955 A255034
Abberley Hall, just behind the clock tower, is now a preparatory school for boys and girls up to the age of 11. Here some boys can be seen having a swimming lesson - although they all seem to be more interested in the photographer, especially the boy who wants to show off his diving skills.

▼ Stanford Bridge, The Bridge and the Post Office c1965 S387014

'Stanford' means 'the stony ford', so there has obviously been a river crossing here for many centuries. The first bridge was built in 1547, but it has since been replaced by this lovely iron bridge which has the words 'Rebuilt by Worcester County Council 1905' along the side. This bridge, too, has since been replaced, but it survives, now used as a footbridge.

▼ Stanford Bridge, The Post Office c1965 S387017

The new bridge, and the road leading to it, now bypass this part of the village, cutting it off almost completely. Unfortunately, the Bridge Hotel has suffered from the lack of passing trade, and the shop next door has now closed down. Notice the petrol pump beside the hotel's doorway.

▲ Stanford Bridge The Parish Church c1965 S387013

Notice the ladders by the building. Perhaps the workmen are repairing the crenellations along the side of the church. Those on the tower have now disappeared altogether, and the stonework generally is in a very poor state. The church sits on a commanding position a little distance from the village it serves - it replaced a church that was flooded by the artificial lake beside Stanford Court.

◀ Clifton upon Teme
Main Street c1960

C331011

This is a pretty little village with some delightful Georgian buildings surrounding a village green. Notice the old pump under the tree - it still survives. The village might be called Clifton upon Teme, but the name is very inaccurate: in fact, the river is at least a mile away - the original settlers wisely chose a site well above the flood plain.

Tenbury Wells, Kyre House c1955 T22051
At one time Kyre House was a TB hospital, but it closed in the 1960s. Now privately owned, it is being lovingly restored. The oldest part of the building is on the left and dates from the 18th century, but it includes some much earlier stonework surviving from an ancient castle. The layout of the gardens has been attributed to Capability Brown; they have now been opened to the public.

Tenbury Wells, St Michael's College c1955 T22037
Notice the boys playing cricket in the foreground - old boys still come to play a game each year. Now an International College, St Michael's was formerly a choir school. It used to have a famous library of 8,000 books, including the copy of the Messiah used by Handel himself at the first performance; these treasures are now housed in the Bodleian Library in Oxford.

Tenbury Wells
Teme Street c1955 T22053
Tenbury means 'the stronghold on the River Teme'; the river is
crossed by a bridge at the end of the street. The 'Wells' is a later
addition to advertise the mineral waters that were discovered in
1862. The old Pump Room where people used to 'take the
waters' has recently been restored at a cost of around £400,000.
It is quite an enchanting little building.

**Tenbury Wells
Teme Street c1950**

T22015

Notice the lady walking unconcernedly with her dog in the middle of the street, even though there is a car coming along behind her. We could not do that today! Otherwise, this little town has not changed so much over the years - the building at the far end of the street, however, has gone.

Tenbury Wells
Teme Street c1955 T22061
Today, people no longer take the waters; instead, Tenbury is best known for its sales of holly and mistletoe just before Christmas each year. Mistletoe grows best on apple trees, and Tenbury has the delightful nickname of 'the town in the orchard'.

Tenbury Wells, Market Street c1950 T22019
One of the oldest buildings in Tenbury is the Royal Oak pub, which is the decorative black and white building in the centre of this photograph. Notice the building further down the street: it is known as the Clock House, and a round, white clock (which still survives) can be seen on the wall.

Tenbury Wells, The Butter Market c1960 T22088
The Butter Market was used to sell not just butter but any other commodities that the farmers' wives could sell while their husbands attended the main markets in the town. There are a number of old posters sticking to the walls - these days there is a discreet sign which tells us that 'Bill Posting is now Prohibited'.

Tenbury Wells, The Cottage Hospital c1955 T22044
In these days when so many small cottage hospitals have been forced to close down, it is good to see that some have survived. The building today looks much the same. It is just possible to make out beds in the open portico behind the gate where patients are getting some fresh air. Today this is inside the hospital, as permanent windows have been inserted.

Tenbury Wells, The Talbot Hotel, Newnham Bridge c1950 T22021
Notice that the sign mentions 'good fishing' - many holidaymakers staying here would have come to the area for the fishing. A talbot was a breed of dog that has now disappeared. It was white with black spots, and had a remarkable sense of smell, and so was used for hunting and tracking. Modern fox hounds are a descendent of the talbot.

The Malvern Hills and the Southern Reaches of the River Severn

Worcester
The Malvern Hills from the Cathedral Tower c1960 W141080
This is a lovely view, taken from the Cathedral looking across the River Severn towards the Malvern Hills to the south-west. The composer Edward Elgar was born just north of the Malverns and grew up in Worcester, but it was the 'English Alps' that were the inspiration for much of his music. He died in 1934, and is buried in Little Malvern.

**Malvern Link
Worcester Road
c1955** M17045
This is the road linking
the various towns and
villages of Malvern with
the county's capital at
Worcester. Malvern
Link is associated with
a very specialised
motor industry - the
production of Morgan
cars. Morgan's is one
of Britain's few
independent car
manufacturers still to
survive, and there is
always a waiting list for
their hand-made sports
cars.

◀ **Great Malvern Church Street c1955**
M17036
Church Street is so named because it lies next to the church yard of 'the most magnificent parish church in England'. The former Benedictine priory was dissolved by Henry VIII, but fortunately for posterity, the church was bought by the townspeople (for the enormous sum of £20) to replace their old parish church.

◀ Great Malvern
Belle Vue Terrace and Church
Street c1955 M17031

Notice the street lamp in the photograph: it is said that it was old gas lamps in Malvern that inspired C S Lewis to use a lamp post in his tales of Narnia. The position of the flagpole in the photograph has since been taken over by a statue and memorial to another local artistic connection, Edward Elgar; otherwise the view has changed little.

▼ Great Malvern
The British Camp Hotel c1950
M17006

The Malvern Hills (the name means 'bare hills') have long attracted visitors, and some of them have stayed here. Notice the gatehouse and driveway on the right: this is the entrance to Wynds Point, the home of Jenny Lind. Better known as 'the Swedish Nightingale', she was one of the greatest singers of the 19th century. She died in 1887, and is buried in Great Malvern.

◀ Great Malvern
The Swimming Pool
the British Camp Hotel
c1955 M17015

After a hard day's walking in the hills, what better way could there be to relax than swimming and lounging by the hotel pool? It has gone now, though. The British Camp Hotel was named for an ancient hillfort on one of the nearby summits. However, since the early 1980s, it has been known as the Malvern Hills Hotel.

▼ **Castlemorton, The Cottage c1960** C499005
The castle that gave this village its name has long since disappeared. The lovely thatched house here is one of a number of lovely homes to be found in the area. Birtsmorton, a mile or so south of here, was the home of William Huskisson, the first man to be killed in an English railway accident; he was knocked over by Stephenson's Rocket in 1830.

▼ **Upton-on-Severn, The Church Tower c1960** U12035
Known locally as the Pepperpot, this is all that remains of the town's medieval church, which was destroyed during the Civil War. The cupola on the top of the tower, though, dates from the 18th century. Today the building houses a Heritage Centre for the town.

▲ **Upton-on-Severn The View from the Bridge c1955** U12014
This area has been a regular haunt for holidaymakers for many years, and it would appear that the coach on the right has brought a number of day trippers to visit the town. Boats are still moored by the river bank, but these days they are large pleasure boats. There are also many private boats here, which are kept in a nearby marina.

◀ **Upton-on-Severn
The White Swan Hotel
c1955** U12019
'Upton' means 'the settlement on higher ground'. But the landlord of the Swan, as it is now called, would probably tell you that the town is not high enough. Whenever the River Severn floods, which it does regularly, the water invariably enters this building.

Upton-on-Severn High Street c1955

U12022

There are some charming buildings in Upton. Many are probably much older than they at first appear, since the old timber buildings have often been covered with later stucco or brickwork. One of the timber buildings that has survived in its original state is pictured here. The Olde Anchor Inn, as it now is, dates from 1601.

Upton-on-Severn
High Street c1955 U12010
Notice the White Lion Hotel: it was mentioned in Henry
Fielding's 'Tom Jones'. The white lion over the entrance now has a
magnificent golden mane. There is a delightful epitaph in the
town, which reads: 'Beneath this stone, in hope of Zion, Doth lie
the landlord of the Lion, His son keeps on the business still,
Resigned unto the heavenly will'.

Longdon
The School c1965 L217010
Notice all the parents, some with children in prams and pushchairs, waiting by the roadside. They are obviously waiting for the children to come out of the primary school, the building on the left with the long sloping roof.

◀ **Bushley
The Village c1960**
B426025
This view has not changed at all in the last 40 years. We are almost in Gloucestershire here, just about as far south as is possible within Worcestershire.

Longdon
The Post Office Stores
c1965 L217001

This petrol station has now disappeared, and its land has been absorbed into the garden of the white house behind. Even the old shop part of the garage has been taken over by the house, and it is all protected from the road by a wall.

Bredon, Church Street and the Post Office
c1955 B423001

The village of Bredon is best known for its magnificent 14th-century tithe barn, which is now maintained by the National Trust. Here we are in the heart of the village - notice the man in the white coat standing beside his delivery van.

Bredon
The Village c1955
B423023

St Giles' church has a lovely spire rising 160 ft. Inside there is a memorial to John Prideaux, a former Bishop of Worcester. A man of moderate views in a time when extreme religious views prevailed, he managed to anger both King and Parliament. Dismissed from office, he came to live here; in the end, he had to sell his precious books to buy food.

Bredon
The Fox and Hounds c1955 B423005
The Fox and Hounds pub is a very popular watering hole. So much
so that it now extends into the brick building next door, as well as
having a conservatory-style extension below the sign, on the wall
behind the young child.

South-Eastern Worcestershire and the Avon Valley

Broadway
The Tower c1955 B222054
The Tower was built in 1797 to take advantage of the superb views of up to 13 counties from the top of Broadway Hill. In the 19th century it was used regularly by William Morris. Today many people can admire the views from here, as the land is now open to the public as a country park.

**Broadway
The Green c1955** ▶
B222055
Broadway is very aptly named - it simply means 'the wide street'. It is not wide enough, though, for modern traffic and the many coachloads of tourists who come to admire this prettiest of Cotswolds villages. Fortunately, a new bypass has just been built, so that relative calm has returned to the village.

◄ **Broadway
The Village c1955**
B222060
Broadway is the 'painted lady of the Cotswolds'. This is a little unfair, as its stone buildings have weathered naturally to their perfect golden colour. The village developed because of the 18th-century stagecoach trade, and numerous inns were established to serve the travellers. The most famous (and expensive!) is the Lygon Arms, the gabled building in the centre of the photograph.

Evesham, Market Square and the Booth Hall c1955 E44069
The Market Square is now totally pedestrianised, but it is still used for an open market every Saturday. The large building at the end of the Square is the Booth Hall, more generally known as the Round House; it dates from the 15th century, and it is currently undergoing restoration.

Evesham, The Booth Hall and the Market Place c1965 E44104
Overlooking the Square is what appears to be the tower of a church. Actually, it is a bell tower, described by Arthur Mee as 'the glory of Evesham'. It was built by Abbot Lichfield only a few years before Evesham's abbey was dissolved by Henry VIII, and would probably have been destroyed had it not been bought by the townspeople.

Evesham
The Booth Hall c1965 E44100
In this photograph the Booth Hall (or the Round House) is the building on the left. Beyond it is Boots the chemists on Bridge Street. This building has since been taken over by the jewellers, F Hinds, and Boots has moved further down Bridge Street, which is now the main shopping area of Evesham.

Evesham ▶
The Abbot's Gateway
c1955 E44064
This delightful gateway is very old indeed - it dates from about 1130 AD. It would originally have linked the old abbey with the town beyond. Notice the iron railings inside the gateway - they are there to protect some wonderful original carved stone arcading. It is interesting, also, to note that the present-day footpath through here is at least 2 ft above the old floor level.

▼ **Evesham, The River and the Bridge c1960** E44079
The old town is surrounded on three sides by the River Avon. Legend tells us that Evesham was named after a swineherd called Eoves, who saw a vision of the Madonna here in 701 AD. He raced to Worcester to tell the Bishop of what he had seen, and so it was decided that a monastery should be built here.

▲ **Evesham**
The Children's Boating
Pool, Abbey Park c1960
E44085
The Abbey was to survive until the reign of Henry VIII, when it was dissolved. The two churches (one for the monks and one for the townspeople) do survive, however, although many of the abbey's buildings were destroyed. The grounds of the abbey now serve as a recreation area for the town.

◀ **Evesham**
Daffodils c1955 E44049
The Vale of Evesham is famous throughout the world for its flowers, fruit and vegetables. Notice how the apple trees in the orchard here all have grease bands to stop pests and insects getting into the fruit that will soon start to form. What a pity this photograph isn't in colour.

▼ South Littleton, High Street c1955 S386003

These immaculately thatched cottages still exist, although they are rather run-down nowadays. Today the three villages of South, Middle and North Littleton all virtually run into each other.

▼ Middle Littleton, The Old Tithe Barn c1960 S386010

This magnificent tithe barn is one of the largest in the country; like the barn at Bredon, it is now looked after by the National Trust. It is 140ft long, and was built in the 14th century. Notice the height of the barn door: it is large enough to enable wagons laden with corn to enter the barn so that they could be unloaded inside.

▲ North Littleton The Village c1960

N220011

This photograph could have been taken 100 years earlier and would have looked just the same. Forty years later, however, and changes have occurred - for example, the thatched roof has been replaced with a tile roof.

◄ **Pebworth**
Pebworth First School
c1960 P171302
Pebworth is as far east as you can go in Worcestershire these days, although until 1931 it was part of the county of Gloucestershire. Here we see the primary school.

▼ **Cleeve Prior, The Green and the Church c1955** C329005
The tree we see here in front of St Andrew's church was an elm that suffered from Dutch elm disease in the 1960s and had to be cut down. It was replaced in 1992 to mark the 40th anniversary of Queen Elizabeth's reign.

▼ **Cleeve Prior, The Green c1960** C329031
This is the view from the tower of the church; we are looking over the village green towards the south-west, with the old elm still in the centre. The scene has hardly changed at all, except that there are now more houses beyond the road. Like so many villages locally, the population has grown considerably in the last few years.

▲ **Cleeve Prior
The Village c1955**
C329004
As we walk around the village it is not at all apparent why it should be named Cleeve or 'cliff'; but in fact the village sits just a short distance away from a steep 200ft cliff overlooking the flood plain of the River Avon. The second element in the name comes because the village once belonged to the Prior of Worcester.

◀ **Cleeve Prior**
The King's Arms c1960

C329035

The King's Arms is typical of 'olde worlde' English pubs in this part of the country. This one dates from the 1400s, although the arms on its sign today are those of Henry VIII. The building on the right is called the Old Cider Mill - most appropriate next to a pub. Notice the child in the pushchair; there's another pram in the courtyard just beyond.

▼ **Cleeve Prior, The Gertrude Myers Convalescent Home c1955** C329010
This convalescent home, which was run by the Birmingham City Council, has now
been closed and the building split into two private houses. It is an unfortunate
sign of the times that so many of these smaller homes are often uneconomic to
run and have had to be closed down.

▼ **Little Comberton, The Village c1955** L216002
There has been a great deal of new housing built here in recent years. This lane,
however, still keeps its old character. Notice the jettied building half-way up the
street - jettying is the name given to upper floors that stick out beyond those
below. It is commonly seen in towns where space was at a premium, but is not
often seen in the villages.

▲ **Little Comberton
The Village c1955**
L216006
What was once three
poor workers' cottages
has now been restored,
and has become a very
up-market residence.
Two of the three doors
survive, and the middle
one has been
transformed into a
window. It is interesting
to note how untidy so
many of our villages were
in the 1950s and 60s
with telegraph poles
everywhere. These
above-ground poles have
now all gone.

◄ **Wyre Piddle**
The Village c1960
W312017
A remarkable survival, considering that it is in the middle of the road junction, is the base and shaft of a medieval wayside cross. The railings have disappeared, however.

◀ **Wyre Piddle**
Old Cottages, Church
Street c1955 W312006
Wyre Piddle is an
extremely pretty little
village serving today as a
dormitory town for
people who work in
Worcester and beyond.
New houses have had to
be built to serve its
growing population, and
although these timber-
framed buildings have
hardly changed at all over
the years, the land behind
the wall on the right is
now occupied by a
number of new houses.

◄ **Wyre Piddle**
Church Street c1960
W312016
This charming lane is no longer instantly recognisable, as the thatched cottages on the right have all been removed. They have since been replaced by two modern bungalows which sit well back from the road.

▼ **Wyre Piddle**
The Arbour Tree c1955
W312003
Many lone trees in the middle of road junctions were removed completely in the early years of the 20th century. It is interesting to note, though, that if a tree managed to survive into or beyond the 1960s it was usually replaced once it finally came down. This is one such tree; fortunately, there is a new tree growing in its place.

◄ **Wyre Piddle**
The Anchor Inn c1955
W312010
The Anchor Inn is a very popular pub sitting in a wonderful position overlooking the River Avon. Notice the gentleman rowing his boat along the river.

▼ **Wyre Piddle, The River Avon c1960** W312015
There are numerous rivers in England that are called the Avon. This comes about because the word Afon (which is still used in Wales today) was simply a Celtic word for 'river': invading Anglo-Saxons, when they asked the name of an individual river, were told that it was just called 'the River'.

▼ **Pershore, The Abbey c1955** P45005
Pershore is thought to mean the 'bank where osiers grow'; osiers were used in basket making. This trade must have brought great prosperity to the settlement, because an abbey was founded here in the 7th century. Even today, with much of it destroyed in the 16th century, it is still 'one of the finest churches in the Midlands'.

▲ **Pershore**
The View from the Abbey Tower c1960
P45074
This view looks north-east towards the High Street (horizontally across the photograph) and the River Avon beyond. The church in the foreground, St Andrew's church, still exists as a building, but it is now redundant as a church; it is used instead as a parish hall.

◀ **Pershore
High Street c1960** P45059
The scene here has
changed little over the past
years, although one or two
buildings have been
replaced. The two vans on
the left are parked outside
the shop to which they
belong - the Wireless
Supply Depot - which still
survives; its familiar brown
and yellow vehicles can still
be seen waiting to collect
goods for delivery.

Pershore, Broad Street c1955 P45010
The aptly named Broad Street leads from the main road towards the Abbey. By the 1950s more and more people owned private cars, and open market spaces in towns were rapidly taken over for parking. But some people still had to rely on the buses - there's a neat queue waiting for the bus beside the telephone box on the right of the photograph.

Pershore, The Old and the New Bridges c1960 P45077
If we look carefully at the old medieval bridge on the right, it is evident that the brickwork in the centre differs from the rest. In fact, the centre of the bridge was blown up during the Civil War by Royalists who were retreating from Worcester. Today it is used as a footpath, and most travellers use the modern bridge on the left.

Index

Frith Book Co Titles

www.francisfrith.co.uk

The Frith Book Company publishes over 100 new titles each year. A selection of those currently available are listed below. For latest catalogue please contact Frith Book Co.

Town Books 96 pages, approx 100 photos. County and Themed Books 128 pages, approx 150 photos (unless specified). All titles hardback laminated case and jacket except those indicated pb (paperback)

Amersham, Chesham & Rickmansworth (pb)	1-85937-340-2	£9.99
Ancient Monuments & Stone Circles	1-85937-143-4	£17.99
Aylesbury (pb)	1-85937-227-9	£9.99
Bakewell	1-85937-113-2	£12.99
Barnstaple (pb)	1-85937-300-3	£9.99
Bath (pb)	1-85937419-0	£9.99
Bedford (pb)	1-85937-205-8	£9.99
Berkshire (pb)	1-85937-191-4	£9.99
Berkshire Churches	1-85937-170-1	£17.99
Blackpool (pb)	1-85937-382-8	£9.99
Bognor Regis (pb)	1-85937-431-x	£9.99
Bournemouth	1-85937-067-5	£12.99
Bradford (pb)	1-85937-204-x	£9.99
Brighton & Hove(pb)	1-85937-192-2	£8.99
Bristol (pb)	1-85937-264-3	£9.99
British Life A Century Ago (pb)	1-85937-213-9	£9.99
Buckinghamshire (pb)	1-85937-200-7	£9.99
Camberley (pb)	1-85937-222-8	£9.99
Cambridge (pb)	1-85937-422-0	£9.99
Cambridgeshire (pb)	1-85937-420-4	£9.99
Canals & Waterways (pb)	1-85937-291-0	£9.99
Canterbury Cathedral (pb)	1-85937-179-5	£9.99
Cardiff (pb)	1-85937-093-4	£9.99
Carmarthenshire	1-85937-216-3	£14.99
Chelmsford (pb)	1-85937-310-0	£9.99
Cheltenham (pb)	1-85937-095-0	£9.99
Cheshire (pb)	1-85937-271-6	£9.99
Chester	1-85937-090-x	£12.99
Chesterfield	1-85937-378-x	£9.99
Chichester (pb)	1-85937-228-7	£9.99
Colchester (pb)	1-85937-188-4	£8.99
Cornish Coast	1-85937-163-9	£14.99
Cornwall (pb)	1-85937-229-5	£9.99
Cornwall Living Memories	1-85937-248-1	£14.99
Cotswolds (pb)	1-85937-230-9	£9.99
Cotswolds Living Memories	1-85937-255-4	£14.99
County Durham	1-85937-123-x	£14.99
Croydon Living Memories	1-85937-162-0	£9.99
Cumbria	1-85937-101-9	£14.99
Dartmoor	1-85937-145-0	£14.99
Derby (pb)	1-85937-367-4	£9.99
Derbyshire (pb)	1-85937-196-5	£9.99
Devon (pb)	1-85937-297-x	£9.99
Dorset (pb)	1-85937-269-4	£9.99
Dorset Churches	1-85937-172-8	£17.99
Dorset Coast (pb)	1-85937-299-6	£9.99
Dorset Living Memories	1-85937-210-4	£14.99
Down the Severn	1-85937-118-3	£14.99
Down the Thames (pb)	1-85937-278-3	£9.99
Down the Trent	1-85937-311-9	£14.99
Dublin (pb)	1-85937-231-7	£9.99
East Anglia (pb)	1-85937-265-1	£9.99
East London	1-85937-080-2	£14.99
East Sussex	1-85937-130-2	£14.99
Eastbourne	1-85937-061-6	£12.99
Edinburgh (pb)	1-85937-193-0	£8.99
England in the 1880s	1-85937-331-3	£17.99
English Castles (pb)	1-85937-434-4	£9.99
English Country Houses	1-85937-161-2	£17.99
Essex (pb)	1-85937-270-8	£9.99
Exeter	1-85937-126-4	£12.99
Exmoor	1-85937-132-9	£14.99
Falmouth	1-85937-066-7	£12.99
Folkestone (pb)	1-85937-124-8	£9.99
Glasgow (pb)	1-85937-190-6	£9.99
Gloucestershire	1-85937-102-7	£14.99
Great Yarmouth (pb)	1-85937-426-3	£9.99
Greater Manchester (pb)	1-85937-266-x	£9.99
Guildford (pb)	1-85937-410-7	£9.99
Hampshire (pb)	1-85937-279-1	£9.99
Hampshire Churches (pb)	1-85937-207-4	£9.99
Harrogate	1-85937-423-9	£9.99
Hastings & Bexhill (pb)	1-85937-131-0	£9.99
Heart of Lancashire (pb)	1-85937-197-3	£9.99
Helston (pb)	1-85937-214-7	£9.99
Hereford (pb)	1-85937-175-2	£9.99
Herefordshire	1-85937-174-4	£14.99
Hertfordshire (pb)	1-85937-247-3	£9.99
Horsham (pb)	1-85937-432-8	£9.99
Humberside	1-85937-215-5	£14.99
Hythe, Romney Marsh & Ashford	1-85937-256-2	£9.99

Available from your local bookshop or from the publisher

Frith Book Co Titles (continued)

Ipswich (pb)	1-85937-424-7	£9.99	St Ives (pb)	1-85937415-8	£9.99
Ireland (pb)	1-85937-181-7	£9.99	Scotland (pb)	1-85937-182-5	£9.99
Isle of Man (pb)	1-85937-268-6	£9.99	Scottish Castles (pb)	1-85937-323-2	£9.99
Isles of Scilly	1-85937-136-1	£14.99	Sevenoaks & Tunbridge	1-85937-057-8	£12.99
Isle of Wight (pb)	1-85937-429-8	£9.99	Sheffield, South Yorks (pb)	1-85937-267-8	£9.99
Isle of Wight Living Memories	1-85937-304-6	£14.99	Shrewsbury (pb)	1-85937-325-9	£9.99
Kent (pb)	1-85937-189-2	£9.99	Shropshire (pb)	1-85937-326-7	£9.99
Kent Living Memories	1-85937-125-6	£14.99	Somerset	1-85937-153-1	£14.99
Lake District (pb)	1-85937-275-9	£9.99	South Devon Coast	1-85937-107-8	£14.99
Lancaster, Morecambe & Heysham (pb)	1-85937-233-3	£9.99	South Devon Living Memories	1-85937-168-x	£14.99
Leeds (pb)	1-85937-202-3	£9.99	South Hams	1-85937-220-1	£14.99
Leicester	1-85937-073-x	£12.99	Southampton (pb)	1-85937-427-1	£9.99
Leicestershire (pb)	1-85937-185-x	£9.99	Southport (pb)	1-85937-425-5	£9.99
Lincolnshire (pb)	1-85937-433-6	£9.99	Staffordshire	1-85937-047-0	£12.99
Liverpool & Merseyside (pb)	1-85937-234-1	£9.99	Stratford upon Avon	1-85937-098-5	£12.99
London (pb)	1-85937-183-3	£9.99	Suffolk (pb)	1-85937-221-x	£9.99
Ludlow (pb)	1-85937-176-0	£9.99	Suffolk Coast	1-85937-259-7	£14.99
Luton (pb)	1-85937-235-x	£9.99	Surrey (pb)	1-85937-240-6	£9.99
Maidstone	1-85937-056-x	£14.99	Sussex (pb)	1-85937-184-1	£9.99
Manchester (pb)	1-85937-198-1	£9.99	Swansea (pb)	1-85937-167-1	£9.99
Middlesex	1-85937-158-2	£14.99	Tees Valley & Cleveland	1-85937-211-2	£14.99
New Forest	1-85937-128-0	£14.99	Thanet (pb)	1-85937-116-7	£9.99
Newark (pb)	1-85937-366-6	£9.99	Tiverton (pb)	1-85937-178-7	£9.99
Newport, Wales (pb)	1-85937-258-9	£9.99	Torbay	1-85937-063-2	£12.99
Newquay (pb)	1-85937-421-2	£9.99	Truro	1-85937-147-7	£12.99
Norfolk (pb)	1-85937-195-7	£9.99	Victorian and Edwardian Cornwall	1-85937-252-x	£14.99
Norfolk Living Memories	1-85937-217-1	£14.99	Victorian & Edwardian Devon	1-85937-253-8	£14.99
Northamptonshire	1-85937-150-7	£14.99	Victorian & Edwardian Kent	1-85937-149-3	£14.99
Northumberland Tyne & Wear (pb)	1-85937-281-3	£9.99	Vic & Ed Maritime Album	1-85937-144-2	£17.99
North Devon Coast	1-85937-146-9	£14.99	Victorian and Edwardian Sussex	1-85937-157-4	£14.99
North Devon Living Memories	1-85937-261-9	£14.99	Victorian & Edwardian Yorkshire	1-85937-154-x	£14.99
North London	1-85937-206-6	£14.99	Victorian Seaside	1-85937-159-0	£17.99
North Wales (pb)	1-85937-298-8	£9.99	Villages of Devon (pb)	1-85937-293-7	£9.99
North Yorkshire (pb)	1-85937-236-8	£9.99	Villages of Kent (pb)	1-85937-294-5	£9.99
Norwich (pb)	1-85937-194-9	£8.99	Villages of Sussex (pb)	1-85937-295-3	£9.99
Nottingham (pb)	1-85937-324-0	£9.99	Warwickshire (pb)	1-85937-203-1	£9.99
Nottinghamshire (pb)	1-85937-187-6	£9.99	Welsh Castles (pb)	1-85937-322-4	£9.99
Oxford (pb)	1-85937-411-5	£9.99	West Midlands (pb)	1-85937-289-9	£9.99
Oxfordshire (pb)	1-85937-430-1	£9.99	West Sussex	1-85937-148-5	£14.99
Peak District (pb)	1-85937-280-5	£9.99	West Yorkshire (pb)	1-85937-201-5	£9.99
Penzance	1-85937-069-1	£12.99	Weymouth (pb)	1-85937-209-0	£9.99
Peterborough (pb)	1-85937-219-8	£9.99	Wiltshire (pb)	1-85937-277-5	£9.99
Piers	1-85937-237-6	£17.99	Wiltshire Churches (pb)	1-85937-171-x	£9.99
Plymouth	1-85937-119-1	£12.99	Wiltshire Living Memories	1-85937-245-7	£14.99
Poole & Sandbanks (pb)	1-85937-251-1	£9.99	Winchester (pb)	1-85937-428-x	£9.99
Preston (pb)	1-85937-212-0	£9.99	Windmills & Watermills	1-85937-242-2	£17.99
Reading (pb)	1-85937-238-4	£9.99	Worcester (pb)	1-85937-165-5	£9.99
Romford (pb)	1-85937-319-4	£9.99	Worcestershire	1-85937-152-3	£14.99
Salisbury (pb)	1-85937-239-2	£9.99	York (pb)	1-85937-199-x	£9.99
Scarborough (pb)	1-85937-379-8	£9.99	Yorkshire (pb)	1-85937-186-8	£9.99
St Albans (pb)	1-85937-341-0	£9.99	Yorkshire Living Memories	1-85937-166-3	£14.99

See Frith books on the internet www.francisfrith.co.uk

FRITH PRODUCTS & SERVICES

Francis Frith would doubtless be pleased to know that the pioneering publishing venture he started in 1860 still continues today. A hundred and forty years later, The Francis Frith Collection continues in the same innovative tradition and is now one of the foremost publishers of vintage photographs in the world. Some of the current activities include:

Interior Decoration

Today Frith's photographs can be seen framed and as giant wall murals in thousands of pubs, restaurants, hotels, banks, retail stores and other public buildings throughout the country. In every case they enhance the unique local atmosphere of the places they depict and provide reminders of gentler days in an increasingly busy and frenetic world.

Product Promotions

Frith products are used by many major companies to promote the sales of their own products or to reinforce their own history and heritage. Frith promotions have been used by Hovis bread, Courage beers, Scots Porage Oats, Colman's mustard, Cadbury's foods, Mellow Birds coffee, Dunhill pipe tobacco, Guinness, and Bulmer's Cider.

Genealogy and Family History

As the interest in family history and roots grows world-wide, more and more people are turning to Frith's photographs of Great Britain for images of the towns, villages and streets where their ancestors lived; and, of course, photographs of the churches and chapels where their ancestors were christened, married and buried are an essential part of every genealogy tree and family album.

Frith Products

All Frith photographs are available Framed or just as Mounted Prints and Posters (size 23 x 16 inches). These may be ordered from the address below. From time to time other products - Address Books, Calendars, Table Mats, etc - are available.

The Internet

Already twenty thousand Frith photographs can be viewed and purchased on the internet through the Frith websites and a myriad of partner sites.

For more detailed information on Frith companies and products, look at these sites:

www.francisfrith.co.uk
www.francisfrith.com
(for North American visitors)

See the complete list of Frith Books at:

www.francisfrith.co.uk

This web site is regularly updated with the latest list of publications from the Frith Book Company. If you wish to buy books relating to another part of the country that your local bookshop does not stock, you may purchase on-line.

For further information, trade, or author enquiries please contact us at the address below:
The Francis Frith Collection, Frith's Barn, Teffont, Salisbury, Wiltshire, England SP3 5QP.
Tel: +44 (0)1722 716 376 Fax: +44 (0)1722 716 881 Email: sales@francisfrith.co.uk

---

See Frith books on the internet www.francisfrith.co.uk

TO RECEIVE YOUR FREE MOUNTED PRINT

Mounted Print
Overall size 14 x 11 inches

Cut out this Voucher and return it with your remittance for £1.95 to cover postage and handling, to UK addresses. For overseas addresses please include £4.00 post and handling. Choose any photograph included in this book. Your SEPIA print will be A4 in size, and mounted in a cream mount with burgundy rule line, overall size 14 x 11 inches.

Order additional Mounted Prints at HALF PRICE (only £7.49 each*)

If there are further pictures you would like to order, possibly as gifts for friends and family, purchase them at half price (no additional postage and handling required).

Have your Mounted Prints framed*

For an additional £14.95 per print you can have your chosen Mounted Print framed in an elegant polished wood and gilt moulding, overall size 16 x 13 inches (no additional postage and handling required).

---

* IMPORTANT!
These special prices are only available if ordered using the original voucher on this page (no copies permitted) and at the same time as your free Mounted Print, for delivery to the same address

---

Frith Collectors' Guild

From time to time we publish a magazine of news and stories about Frith photographs and further special offers of Frith products. If you would like 12 months FREE membership, please return this form.

Send completed forms to:
The Francis Frith Collection, Frith's Barn, Teffont, Salisbury, Wiltshire SP3 5QP

Voucher for **FREE** and Reduced Price Frith Prints

Picture no.	Page number	Qty	Mounted @ £7.49	Framed + £14.95	Total Cost
		1	**Free of charge***	£	£
			£7.49	£	£
			£7.49	£	£
			£7.49	£	£
			£7.49	£	£
			£7.49	£	£

Please allow 28 days for delivery	*** Post & handling**	**£1.95**
Book Title	**Total Order Cost**	**£**

Please do not photocopy this voucher. Only the original is valid, so please cut it out and return it to us.

I enclose a cheque / postal order for £ . . . .
made payable to 'The Francis Frith Collection'
OR please debit my Mastercard / Visa / Switch / Amex card
(credit cards please on all overseas orders)

Number . . . .

Issue No(Switch only) . . . . .Valid from (Amex/Switch) . . . .

Expires . . . .   Signature . . . .

Name Mr/Mrs/Ms . . . .

Address . . . .

. . . .

. . . .

. . . . Postcode . . . .

Daytime Tel No . . . .   Valid to 31/12/03

The Francis Frith Collectors' Guild

Please enrol me as a member for 12 months free of charge.

Name Mr/Mrs/Ms . . . .

Address . . . .

. . . .

. . . .

. . . . Postcode . . . .

Would you like to find out more about Francis Frith?

We have recently recruited some entertaining speakers who are happy to visit local groups, clubs and societies to give an illustrated talk documenting Frith's travels and photographs. If you are a member of such a group and are interested in hosting a presentation, we would love to hear from you.

Our speakers bring with them a small selection of our local town and county books, together with sample prints. They are happy to take orders. A small proportion of the order value is donated to the group who have hosted the presentation. The talks are therefore an excellent way of fundraising for small groups and societies.

Can you help us with information about any of the Frith photographs in this book?

We are gradually compiling an historical record for each of the photographs in the Frith archive. It is always fascinating to find out the names of the people shown in the pictures, as well as insights into the shops, buildings and other features depicted.

If you recognize anyone in the photographs in this book, or if you have information not already included in the author's caption, do let us know. We would love to hear from you, and will try to publish it in future books or articles.

Our production team

Frith books are produced by a small dedicated team at offices in the converted Grade II listed 18th-century barn at Teffont near Salisbury, illustrated above. Most have worked with the Frith Collection for many years. All have in common one quality: they have a passion for the Frith Collection. The team is constantly expanding, but currently includes:

Jason Buck, John Buck, Douglas Burns, Heather Crisp, Lucy Elcock, Isobel Hall, Rob Hames, Hazel Heaton, Peter Horne, James Kinnear, Tina Leary, Hannah Marsh, Eliza Sackett, Terence Sackett, Sandra Sanger, Lewis Taylor, Shelley Tolcher, Helen Vimpany, Clive Wathen and Jenny Wathen.